✳ Smithsonian

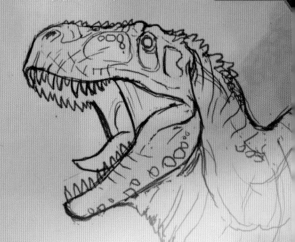

HOW TO DRAW
INCREDIBLE
DINOSAURS

WRITTEN BY KRISTEN MCCURRY

ILLUSTRATED BY JUAN CALLE

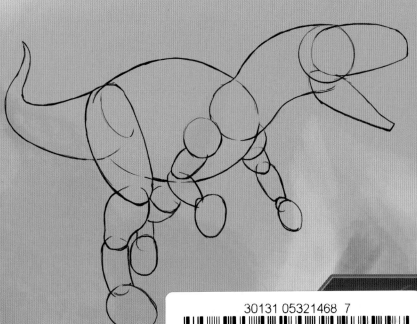

Raintree

TABLE OF CONTENTS

Albertosaurus... 4
Allosaurus.. 6
Ankylosaurus....................................... 8
Brachiosaurus.......................................10
Chungkingosaurus 12
Coelophysis..14
Corythosaurus 16
Deinonychus 18
Diplodocus 20
Edmontonia...22
Edmontosaurus....................................24
Falcarius 26
Gasparinisaura 28
Gastonia 30
Gigantspinosaurus................................32
Kentrosaurus..34

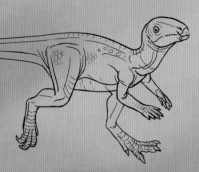

Leaellynasaura 36
Maiasaura 38
Microraptor 40
Omeisaurus...................................... 42
Ouranosaurus 44
Pachycephalosaurus............................ 46
Plateosaurus 48
Rugops.. 50
Stegosaurus 52
Styracosaurus 54
Thescelosaurus................................. 56
Triceratops 58
Tyrannosaurus rex 60
Velociraptor.................................... 62

Websites.. 64

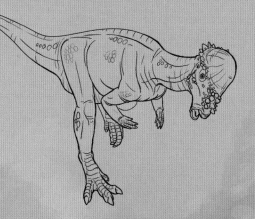

DINOSAUR ERA

TRIASSIC PERIOD
251 MILLION YEARS AGO

JURASSIC PERIOD
199 MILLION YEARS AGO

CRETACEOUS PERIOD
145 to 65 MILLION YEARS AGO

ALBERTOSAURUS
Cretaceous Period

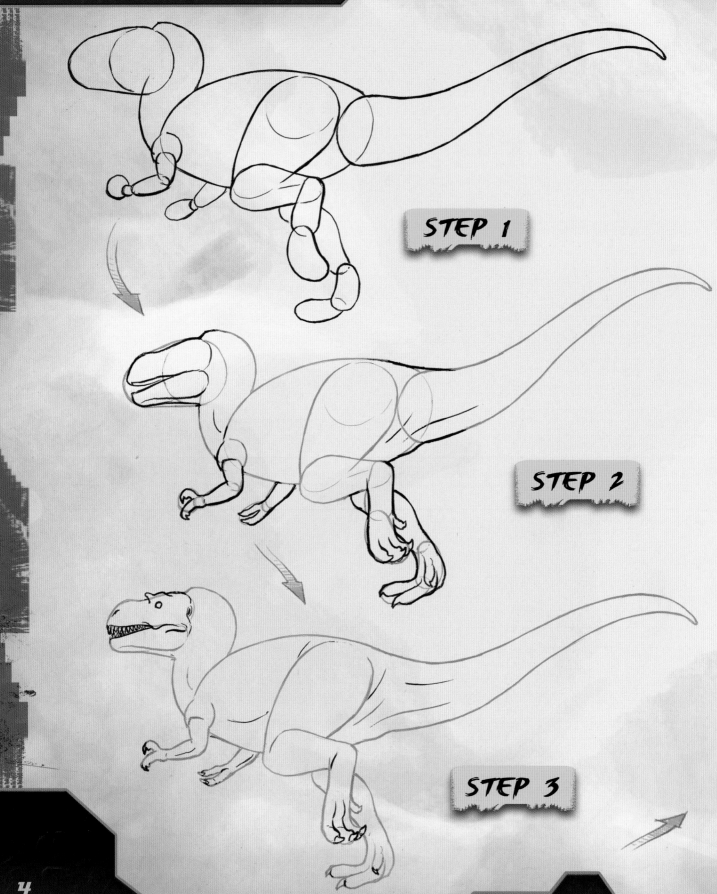

STEP 1

STEP 2

STEP 3

Albertosaurus looked similar to its cousin,
Tyrannosaurus rex, but its powerful body was smaller.
Albertosaurus ate meat and used its curved, serrated
teeth to tear into flesh and bone. It chased live prey
but would also eat dead animals it found.

STEP 4

STEP 5

STEP 1

STEP 2

STEP 3

Allosaurus used its strong back legs to run across the plains after prey. It chased herds of plant-eating animals, singling out a member to kill. Allosaurus had long arms that ended in three claws. Above each eye it had a narrow, raised ridge, which may have been brightly coloured to attract mates.

STEP 4

STEP 5

ANKYLOSAURUS
Cretaceous Period

STEP 1

STEP 2

STEP 3

Ankylosaurus ate plants and was built like a tank. It had a covering of armour over its head, body and tail. Even its eyes had eyelids of bone. Most of the armour was made up of flat bony plates with spikes sticking up. Ankylosaurus' best defence may have been its strong, clubbed tail, which it could swing like a demolition ball.

STEP 4

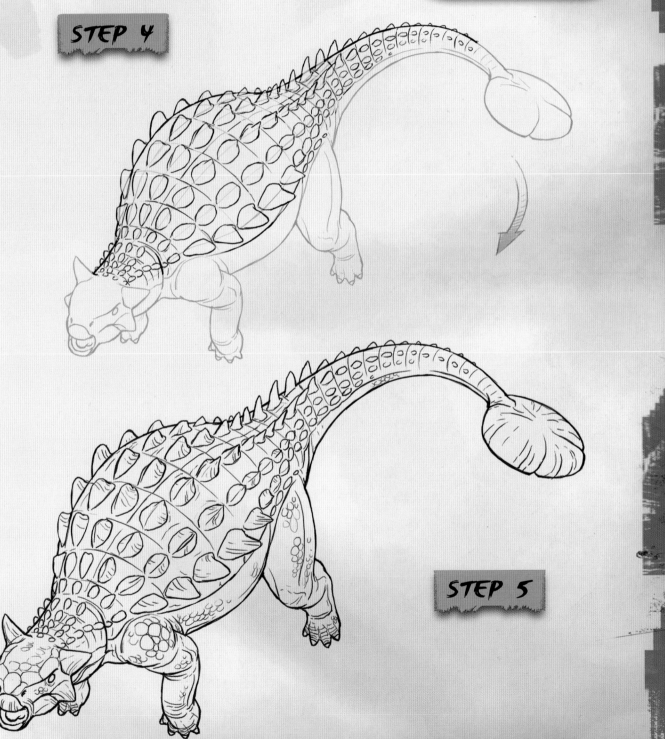

STEP 5

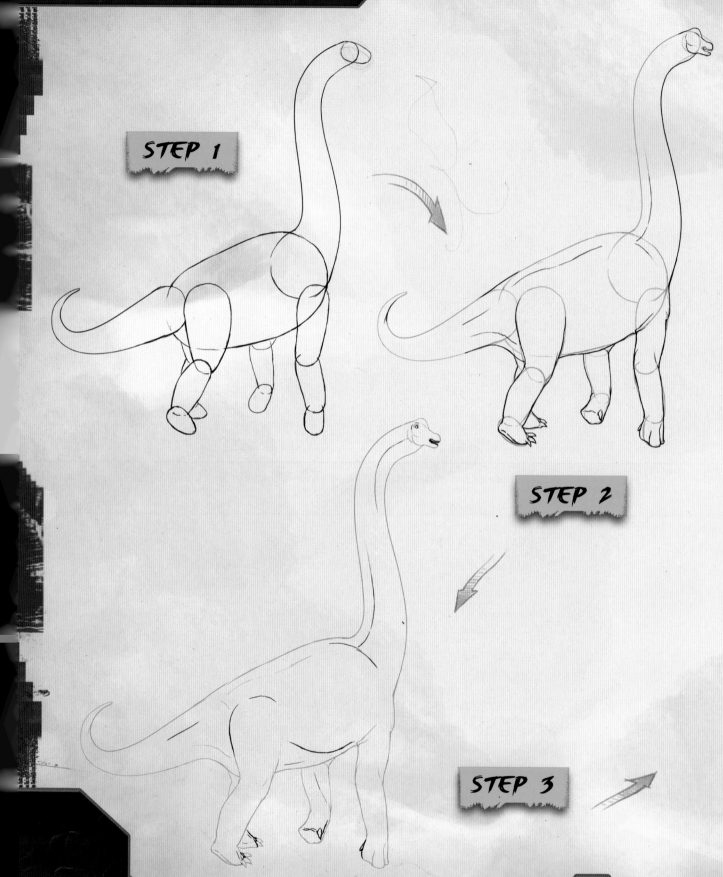

STEP 1

STEP 2

STEP 3

Brachiosaurus was a massive dinosaur that weighed as much as six elephants. Its incredible height allowed it to eat plants that few other creatures could reach. To feed its large body, Brachiosaurus may have needed to eat for more than half of the day.

STEP 4

STEP 5

CHUNGKINGOSAURUS
Jurassic Period

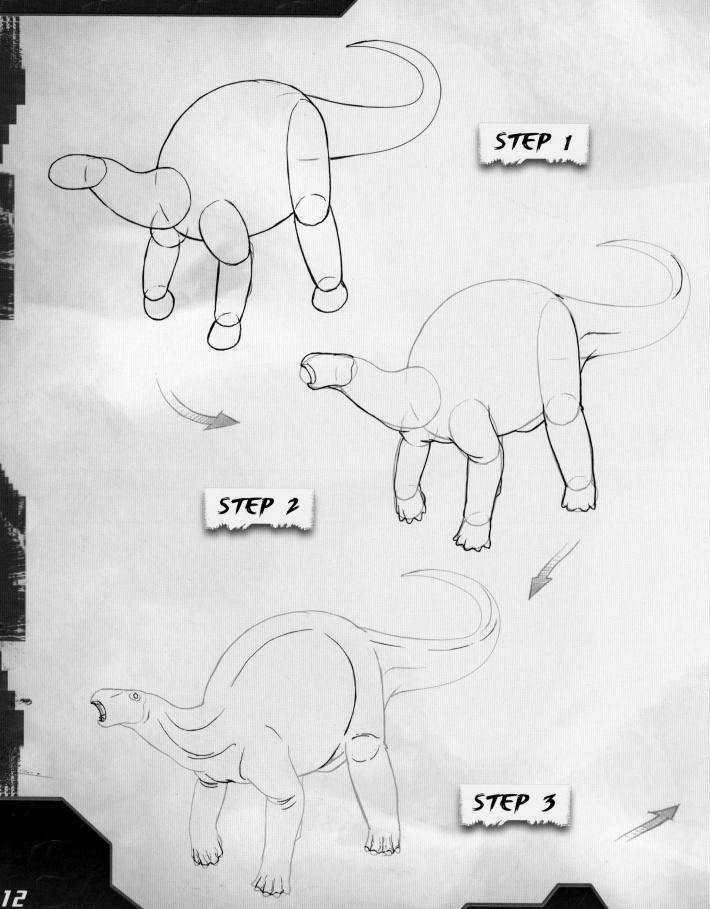

STEP 1

STEP 2

STEP 3

Chungkingosaurus was a small stegosaur that ate plants and was found in China. It had a small head and a double row of spike-like plates running down its back. Scientists believe Chungkingosaurus may have had five sharp spikes at the end of its tail. Other stegosaurs only had four.

STEP 4

STEP 5

STEP 1

STEP 2

STEP 3

Coelophysis was one of the first meat-eating dinosaurs. This small, lightweight hunter travelled in a pack and probably fed on small reptiles and other creatures. Coelophysis was a fast and active predator. It had large eyes and serrated teeth for finding and eating prey.

STEP 4

STEP 5

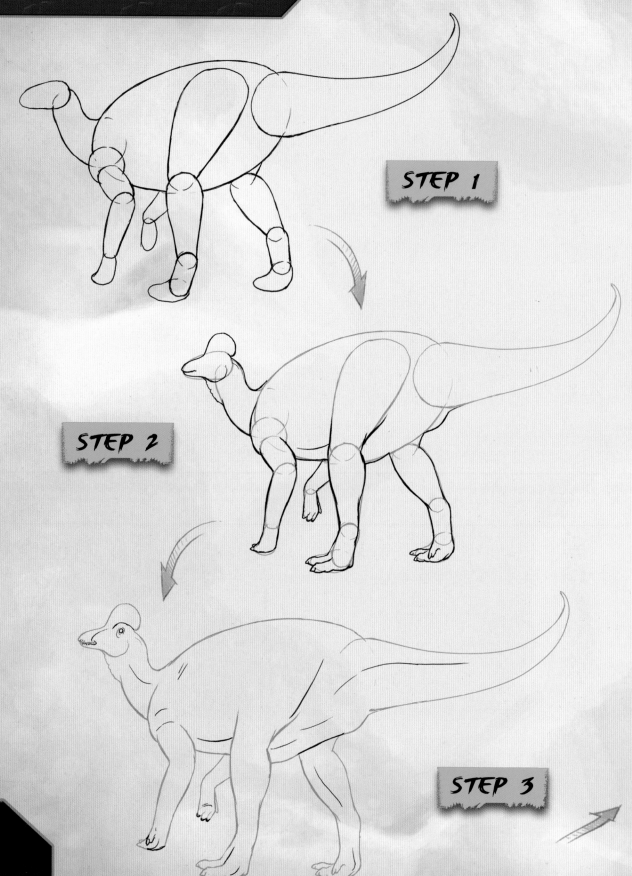

STEP 1

STEP 2

STEP 3

Corythosaurus ate plants, had a duck bill and a large, rounded crest on its head. Scientists believe this crest held a hollow chamber that helped the dinosaur make loud sounds. Corythosaurus had padded hands and short front legs. It walked on all fours but ran on its hind legs.

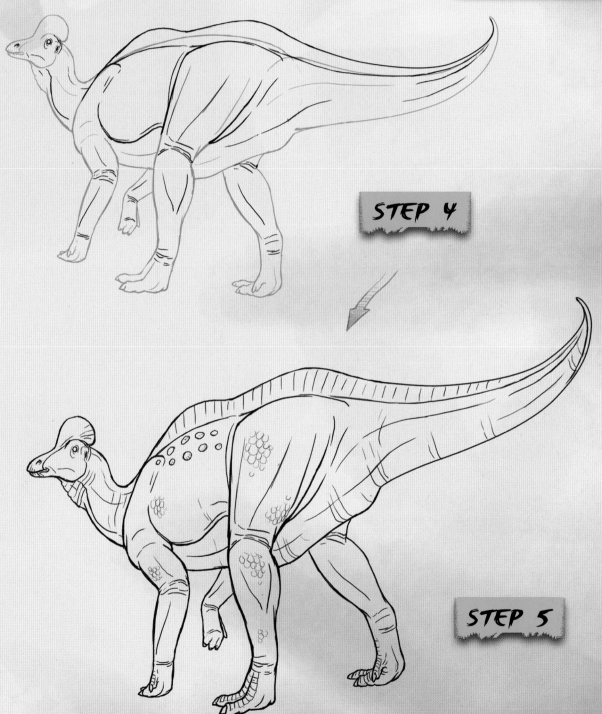

STEP 4

STEP 5

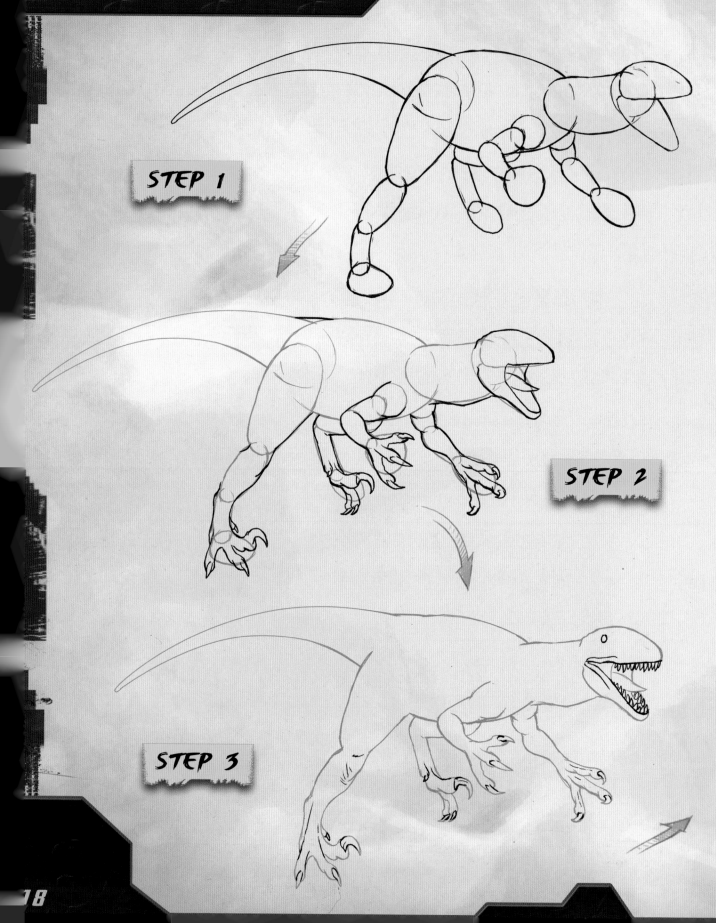

STEP 1

STEP 2

STEP 3

Deinonychus was a fierce pack hunter. It had a large talon on the second toe of each foot that it used to tear meat. In fact, the name Deinonychus means "terrible claw". These small but deadly dinosaurs had relatively large brains and strong eyesight. They preyed on dinosaurs much bigger than themselves.

STEP 4

STEP 5

DIPLODOCUS
Jurassic Period

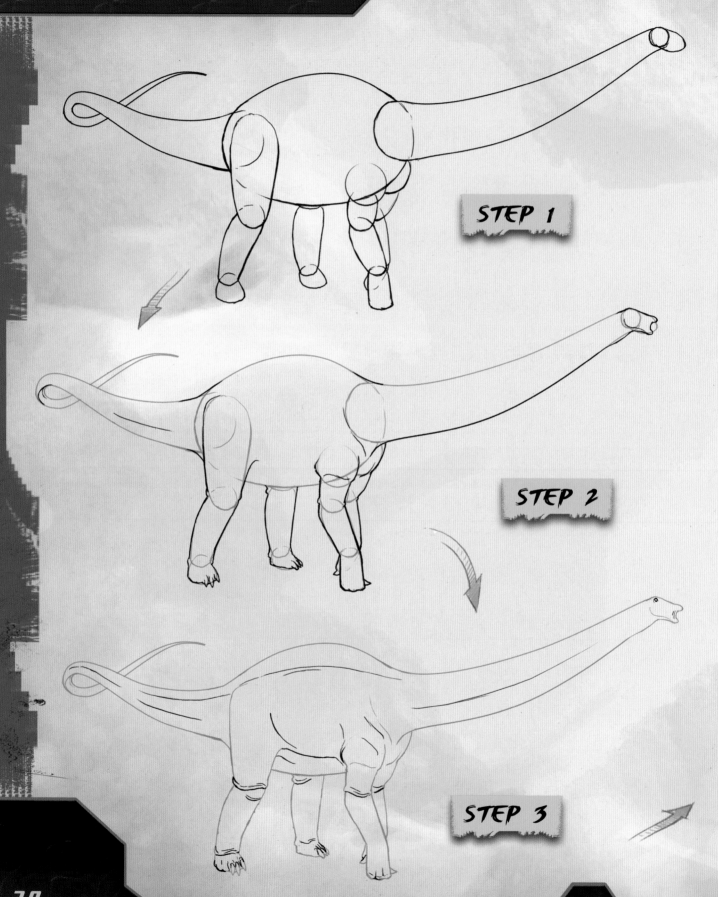

STEP 1

STEP 2

STEP 3

At nearly 27 metres long, Diplodocus was one of the longest land animals in history. Though its neck was very long, Diplodocus moved its head from side to side, eating from plants near the ground or just above its shoulder height.

STEP 4

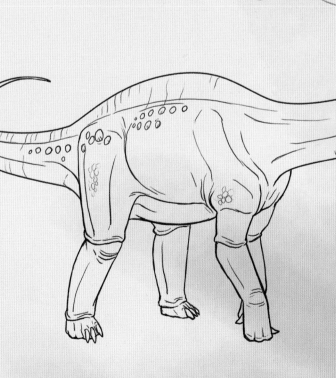

STEP 5

EDMONTONIA
Cretaceous Period

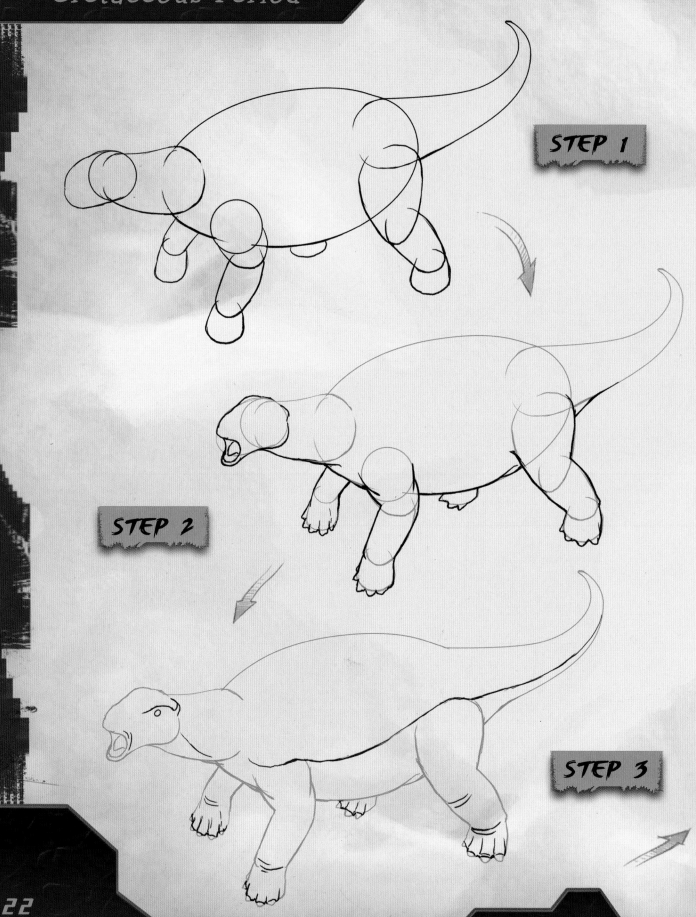

STEP 1

STEP 2

STEP 3

Edmontonia was a short-legged dinosaur with armour on its back and spikes coming out of its sides. These features helped protect it from the huge meat-eating Gorgosaurus and other predators. Edmontonia had a beak that helped it gather plants to eat. Some scientists believe Edmontonia could make honking sounds.

STEP 4

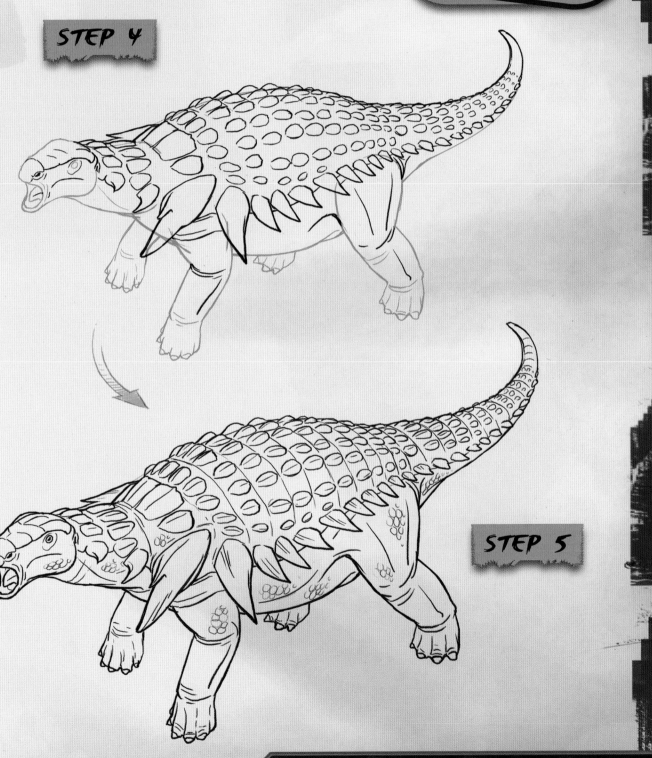

STEP 5

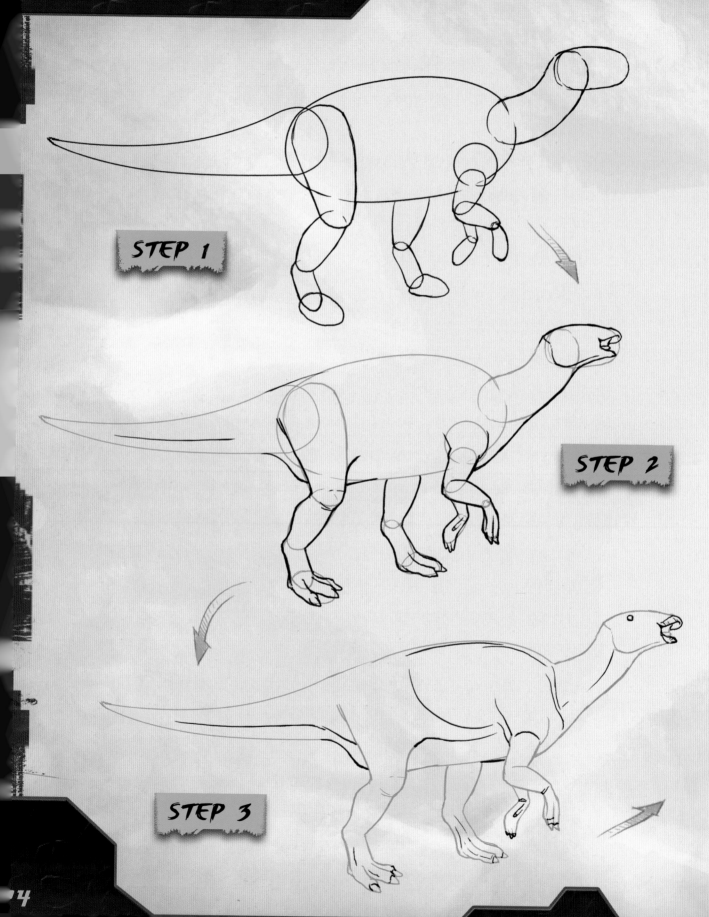

STEP 1

STEP 2

STEP 3

Edmontosaurus could crunch through tough trees and plants with its strong jaw and more than 700 teeth. This dinosaur spent most of its time on land. T-rex was one of its predators, but Edmontosaurus was able to remain safe if it stayed in a herd.

STEP 4

STEP 5

FALCARIUS
Cretaceous Period

STEP 1

STEP 2

STEP 3

Falcarius, one of the raptor dinosaurs, ate both plants and meat. It used its hands to reach for plants and had long, curved claws to strip leaves from their branches. Falcarius had leaf-shaped teeth. It walked on two legs and had a feather-like coating.

STEP 4

STEP 5

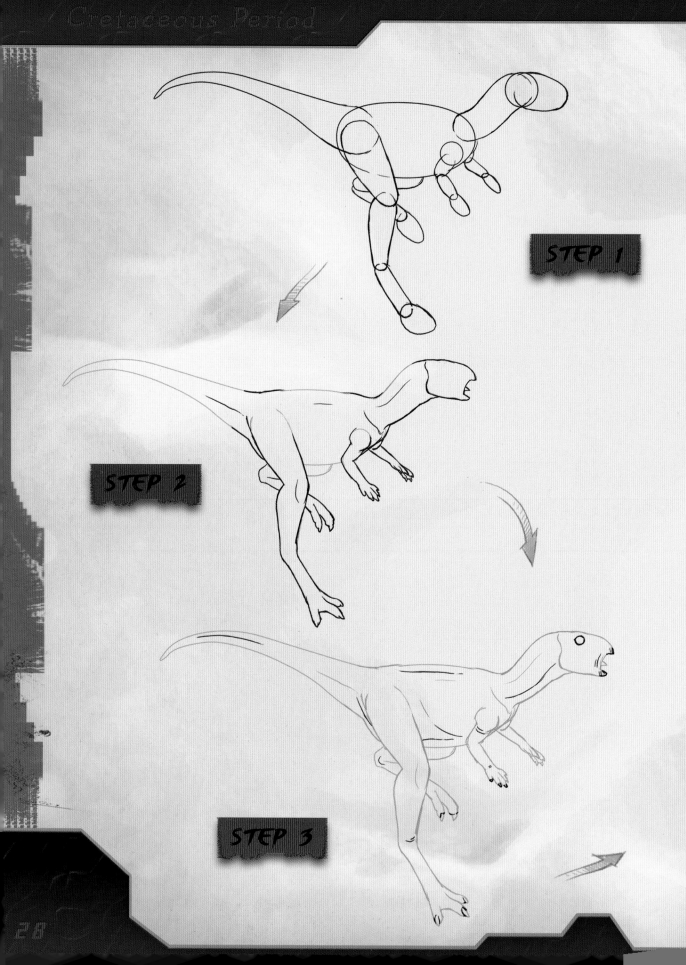

STEP 1

STEP 2

STEP 3

Gasparinisaura was a small dinosaur that may have lived in herds to help protect itself from larger predators. It walked on its powerful hind legs and had very short arms.

STEP 4

STEP 5

GASTONIA
Cretaceous Period

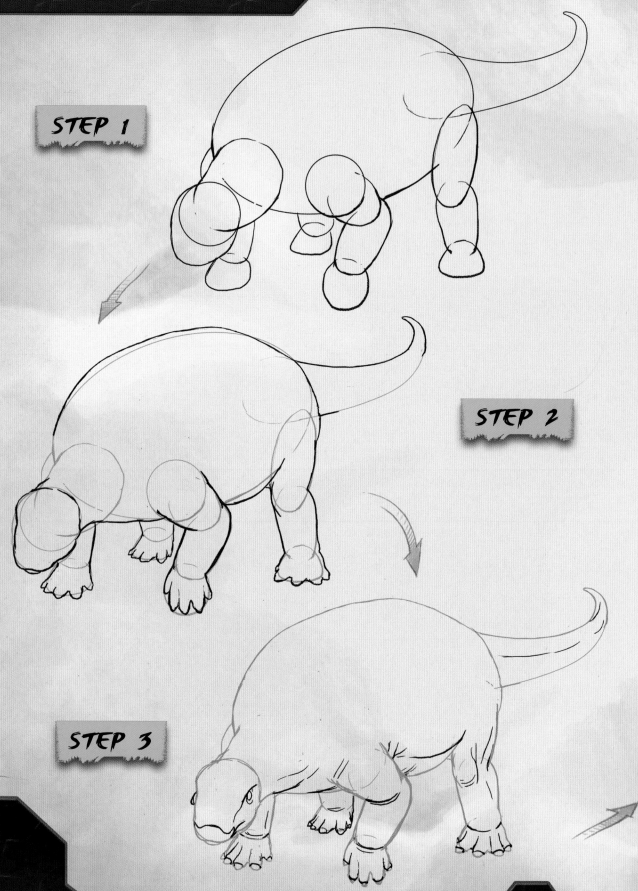

STEP 1

STEP 2

STEP 3

Gastonia was armoured, spiky and ate plants. This dinosaur used its long, sharp spikes for defence against its many predators. Gastonia's short height and stumpy legs made it a slow mover. But these features also helped protect Gastonia's soft underbelly from predators' teeth.

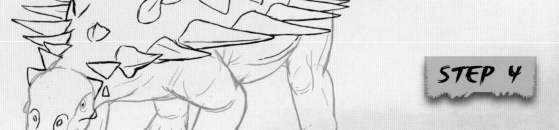

STEP 4

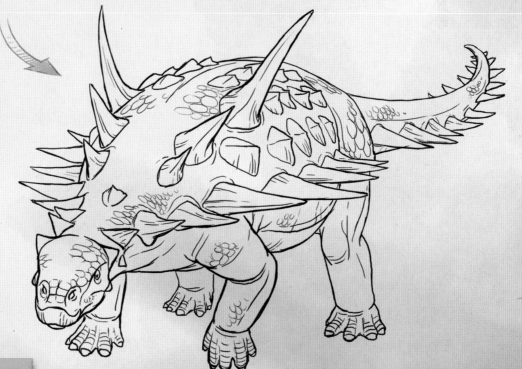

STEP 5

GIGANTSPINOSAURUS

Jurassic Period

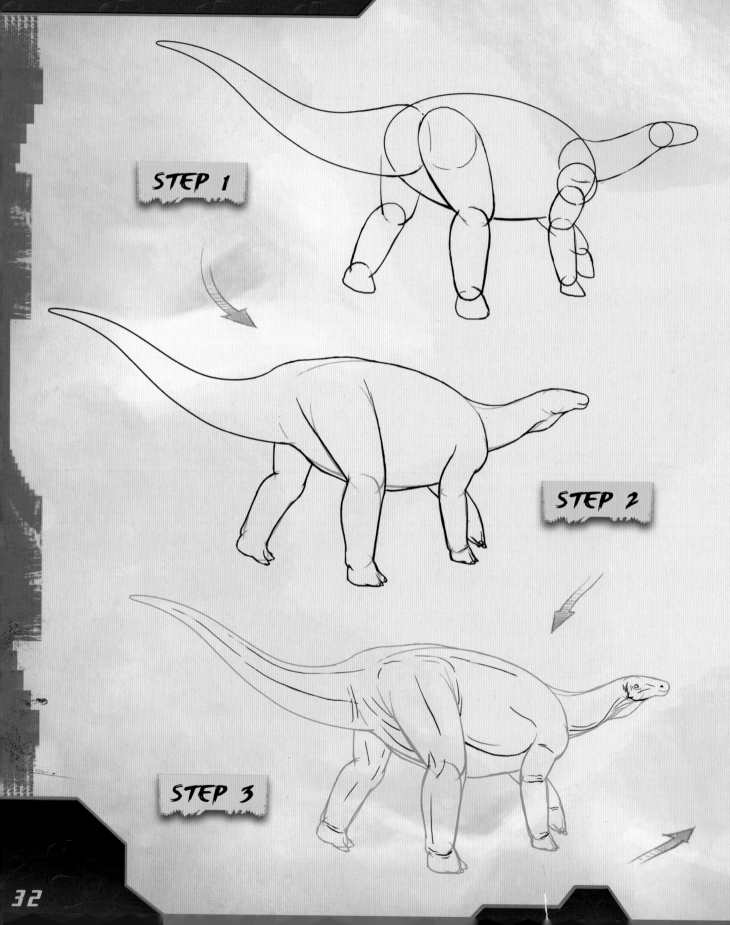

STEP 1

STEP 2

STEP 3

Gigantspinosaurus was a large spiked dinosaur in the stegosaur group. In fact, its name means "giant spined lizard". Two long spikes jutted out from its shoulder blades. It had a small head and was about 4 metres long. Gigantspinosaurus ate plants.

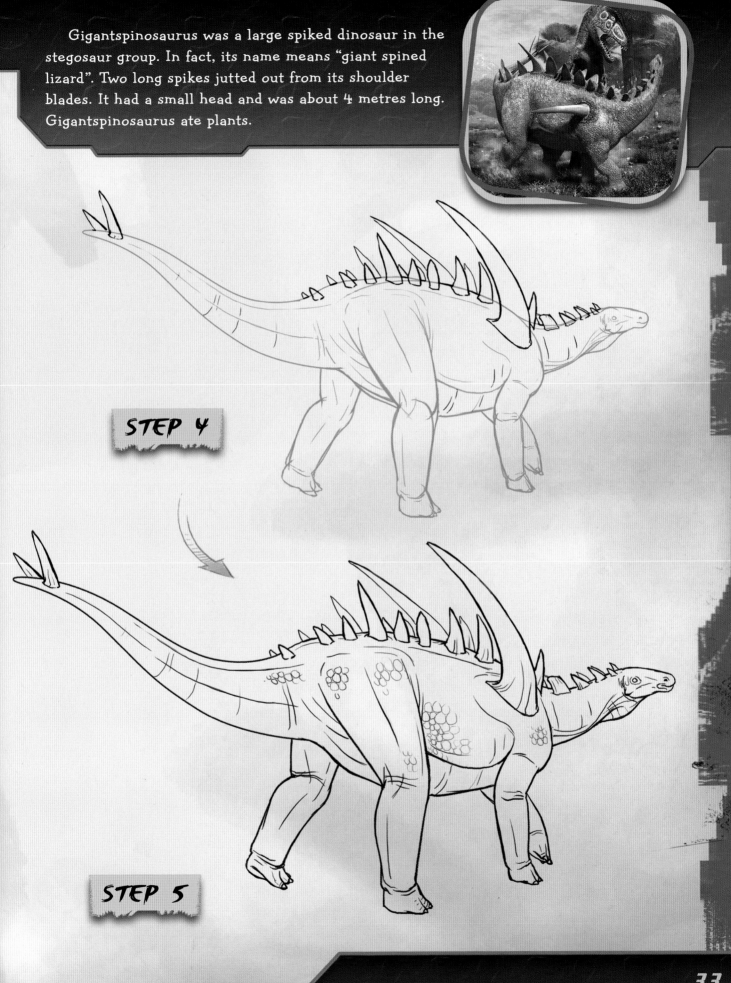

STEP 4

STEP 5

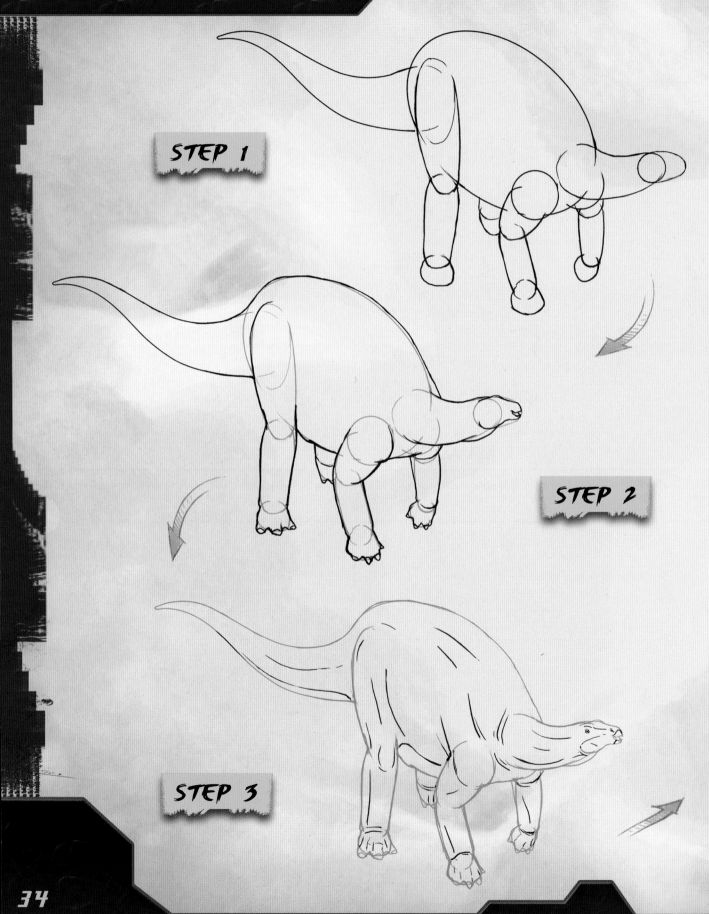

STEP 1

STEP 2

STEP 3

This small stegosaur had large bony plates that ran down its back in pairs and two long spikes over its shoulders. Blood running through the plates on its back helped warm or cool the dinosaur as needed. Kentrosaurus ate plants and was probably hunted by allosaurs.

STEP 4

STEP 5

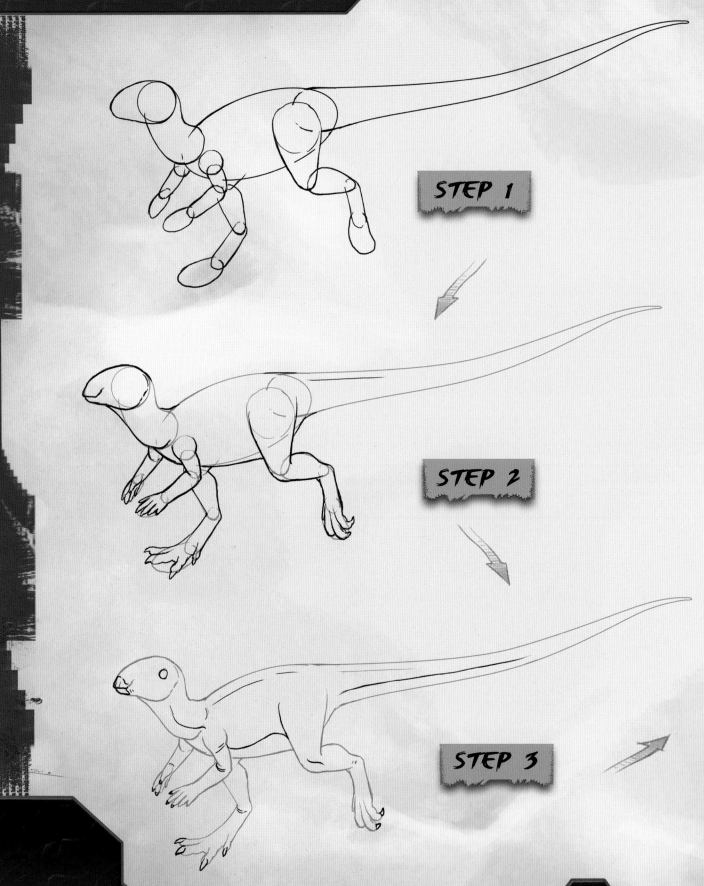

STEP 1

STEP 2

STEP 3

Leaellynasaura was small, ate plants and lived in southern Australia. It may have been warm-blooded to help it survive in the cold. Leaellynasaura had a large brain, which shows that it was intelligent. It also had large eyes that may have helped it to see in the dark winter months.

STEP 4

STEP 5

STEP 1

STEP 2

STEP 3

Maiasaura means "good mother lizard". Scientists gave the duck-billed dinosaur its name because they believe it cared for its young after the eggs hatched. Maiasaura was 9 metres long and ate plants constantly to feed its large body.

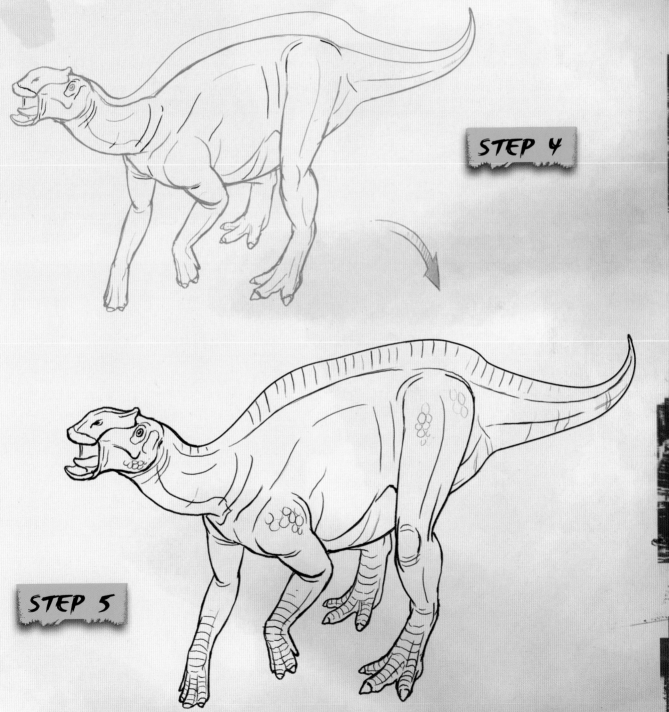

STEP 4

STEP 5

MICRORAPTOR
Cretaceous Period

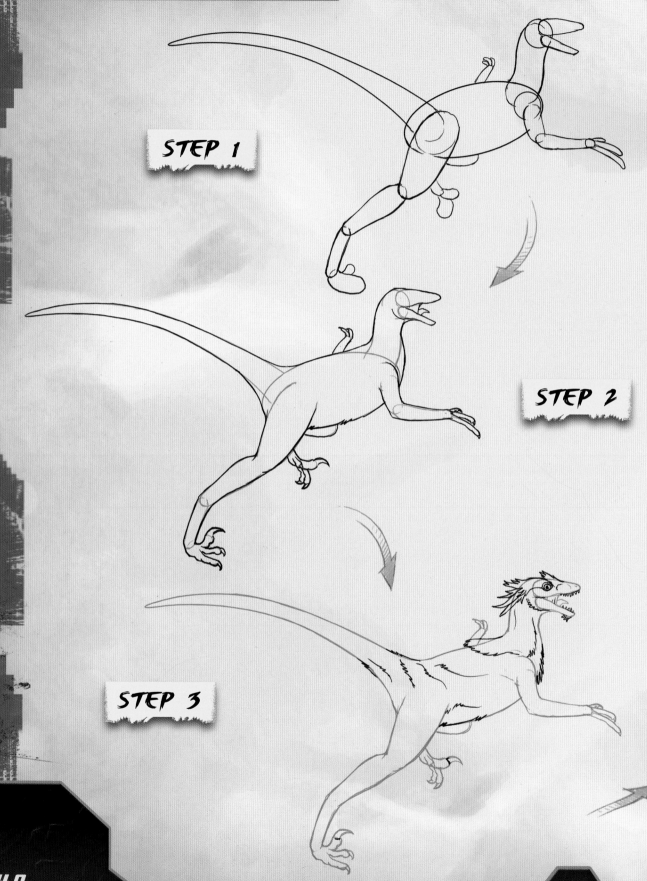

STEP 1

STEP 2

STEP 3

Microraptor was a tiny, feathered dinosaur that weighed only 1.4 to 1.8 kilograms. It had wings on both its arms and legs and was able to glide from tree to tree. Its feathers may have helped keep it warm. Microraptor ate meat. It used a claw on its middle toe for defence.

STEP 4

STEP 5

OMEISAURUS

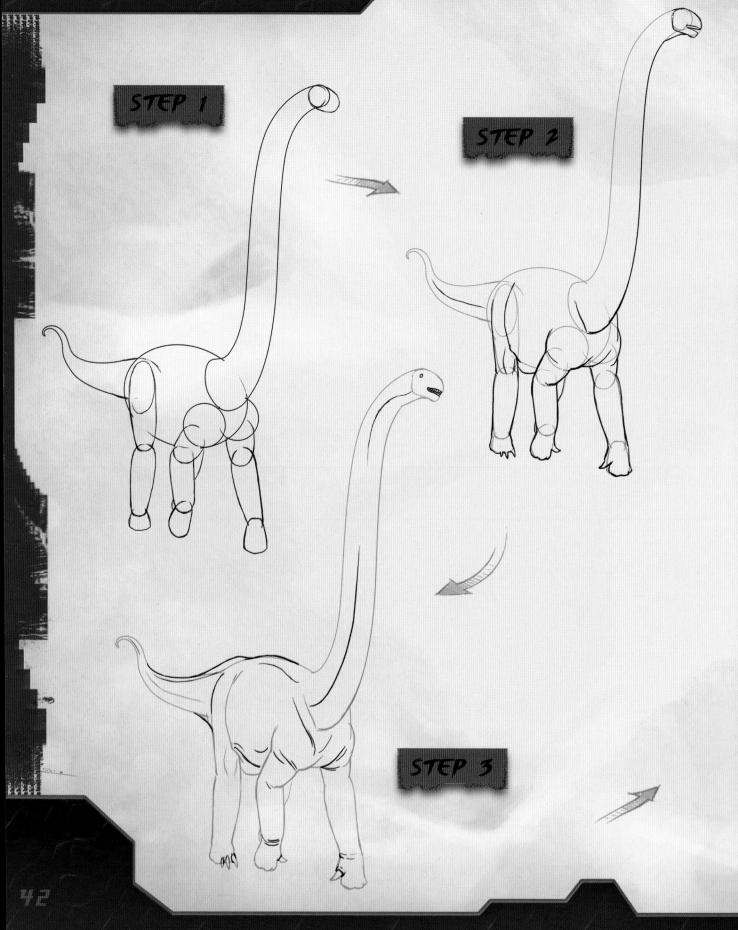

STEP 1

STEP 2

STEP 3

Omeisaurus had one of the longest necks of all the long-necked dinosaurs. Its spoon-shaped teeth helped it eat plants. The adult Omeisaurus probably had few predators because of its incredible size.

STEP 4

STEP 5

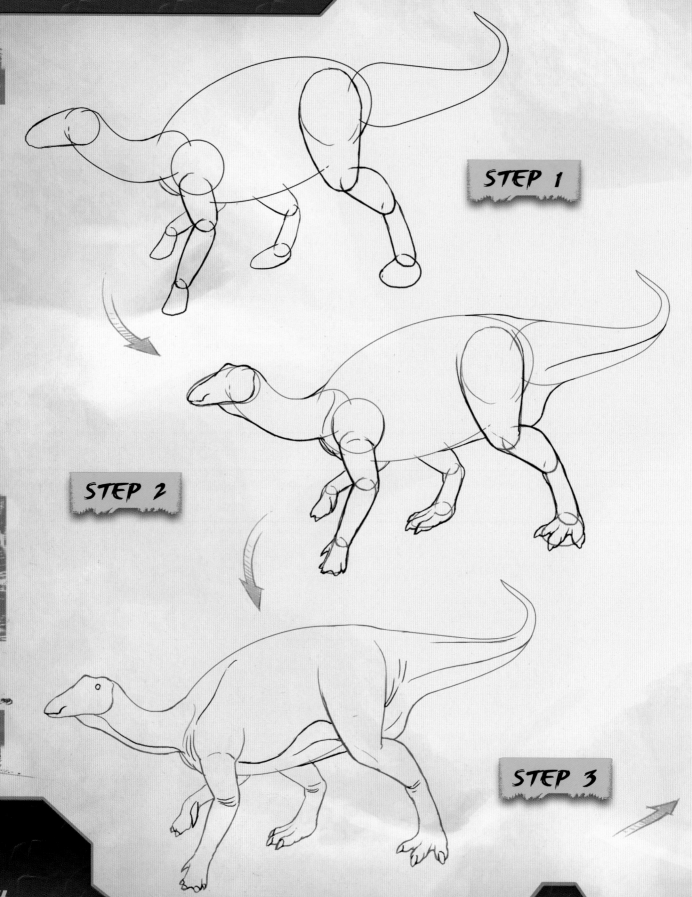

STEP 1

STEP 2

STEP 3

Ouranosaurus had an unusual skeleton. It ate plants and had a large head with long jaws. It may have had a horny beak on the front of its long snout. Ouranosaurus also had a large sail on its back, which may have helped it to stay cool in its desert home.

STEP 4

STEP 5

PACHYCEPHALOSAURUS
Cretaceous Period

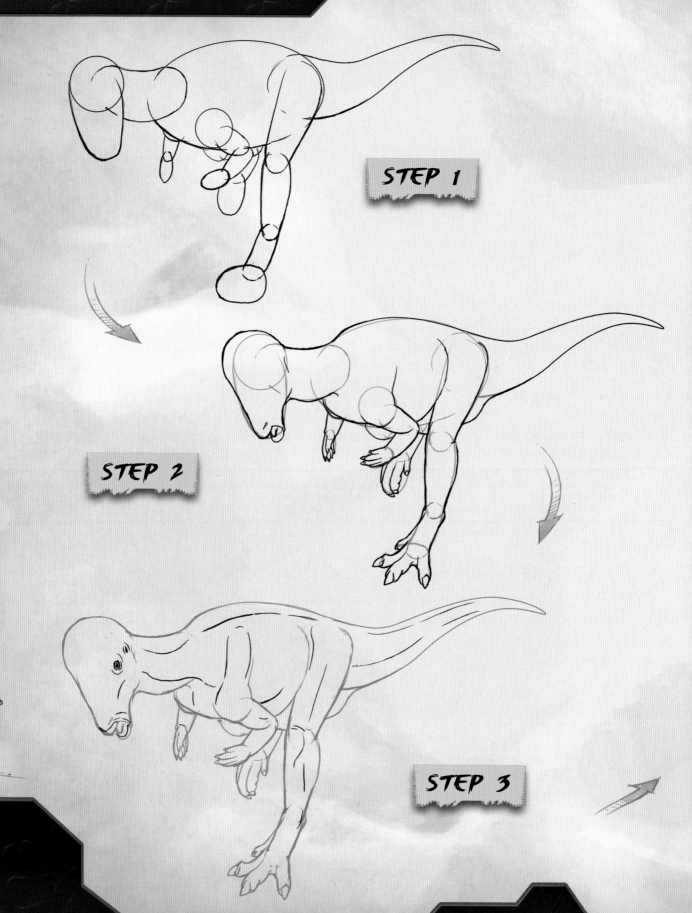

STEP 1

STEP 2

STEP 3

Pachycephalosaurus ate plants and was the largest of the "thick-headed dinosaurs". Its domed head was smooth and round, and the top of its skull could be 23 centimetres thick. It may have engaged in head-butting with other males of its kind.

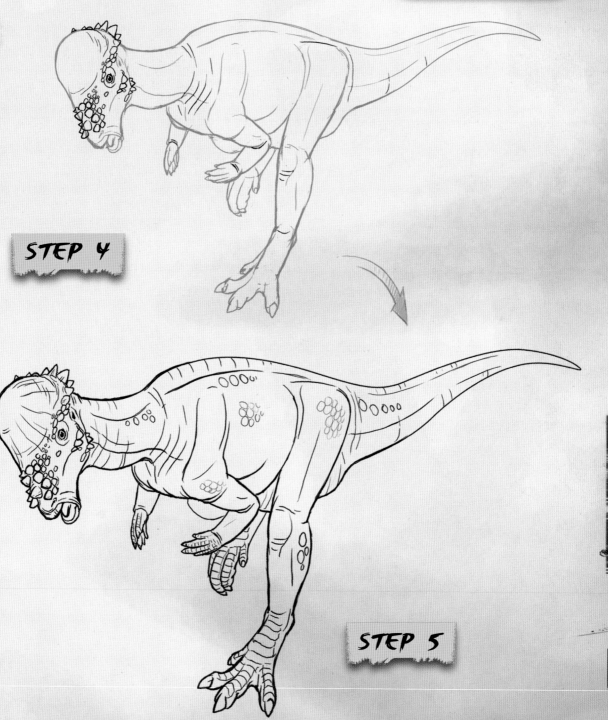

STEP 4

STEP 5

PLATEOSAURUS
Triassic Period

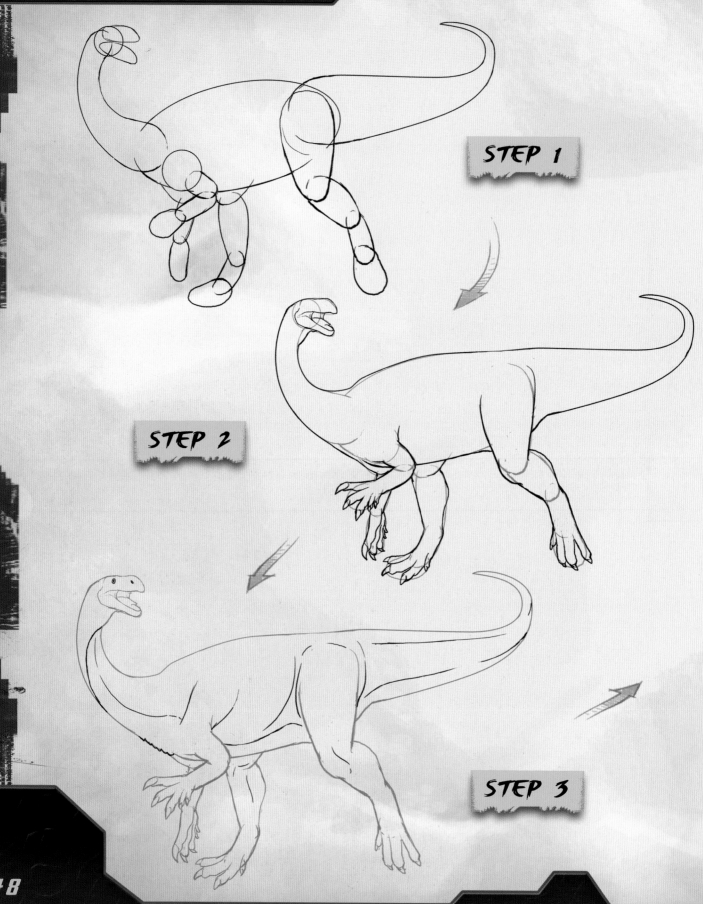

STEP 1

STEP 2

STEP 3

This dinosaur was one of the largest of its time period. Plateosaurus was thought to be able to walk on either two or four legs. It used its long neck and great height to feed off high tree branches. Plateosaurus may have used its clawed thumbs for defence.

STEP 4

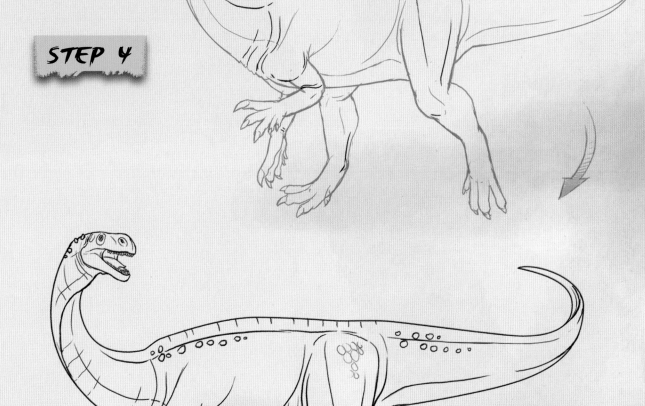

STEP 5

RUGOPS
Cretaceous Period

STEP 1

STEP 2

STEP 3

Rugops means "wrinkle face". This wrinkly faced dinosaur ate meat and had a rounded snout and small teeth. It probably ate animals that were already dead as well as hunting live ones. Rugops had two rows of seven holes on its skull. Scientists believe they may have been from a fleshy crest on the dinosaur's face.

STEP 4

STEP 5

STEGOSAURUS
Jurassic Period

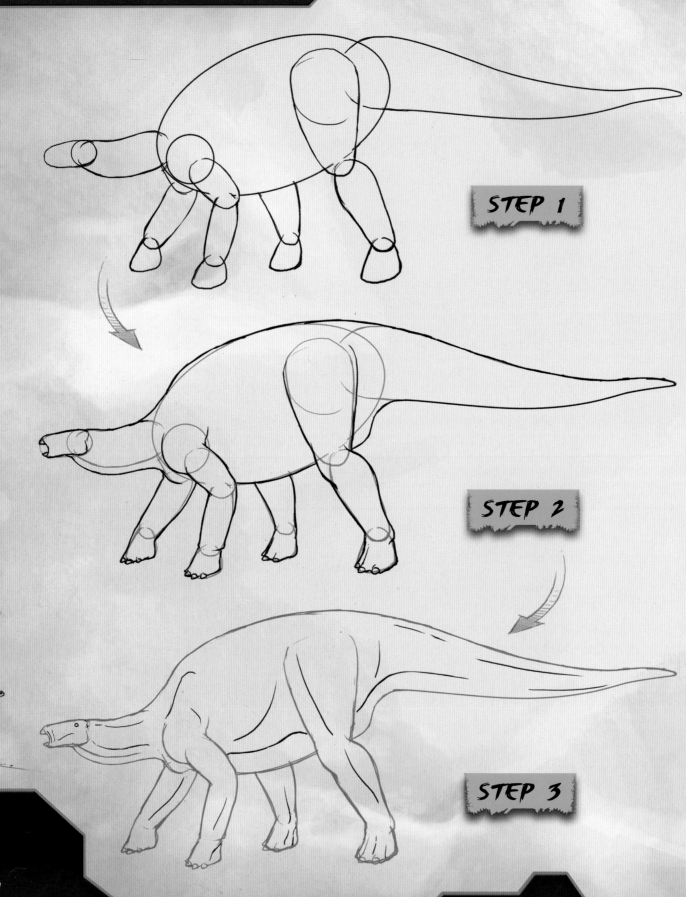

STEP 1

STEP 2

STEP 3

Stegosaurus ate plants. It had two rows of large bony plates running down its back. At the end of its tail it had two pairs of spikes. These spikes may have been for defence. Stegosaurus had a small brain, but good armour. Armoured bumps in the skin under its neck may have protected it from predators.

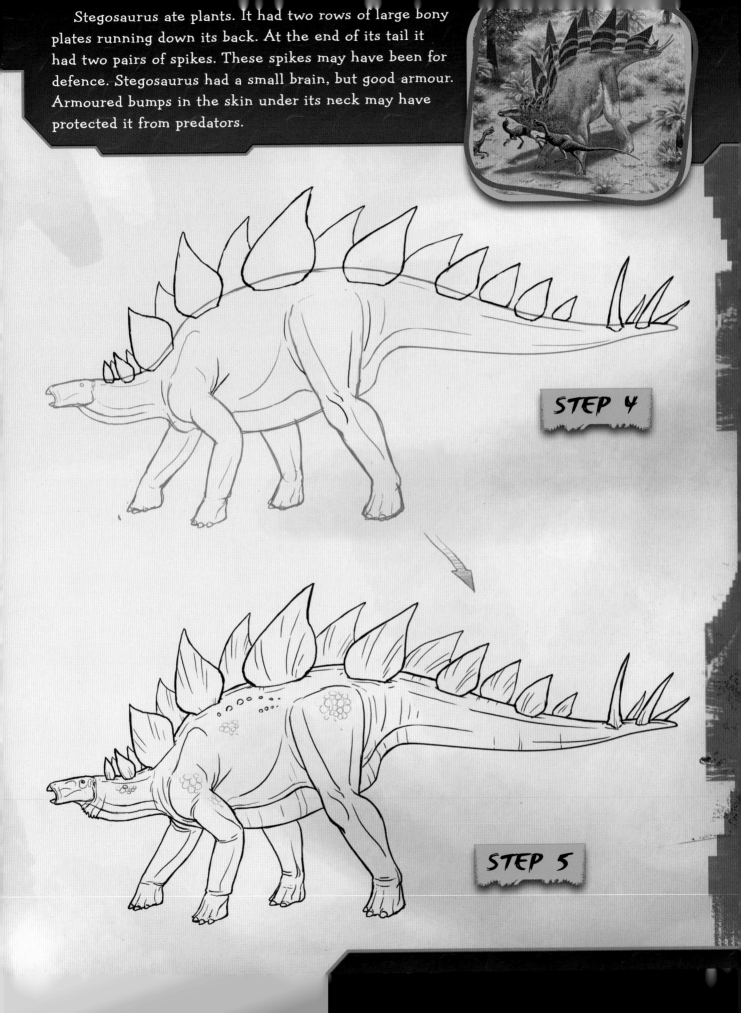

STEP 4

STEP 5

STYRACOSAURUS
Cretaceous Period

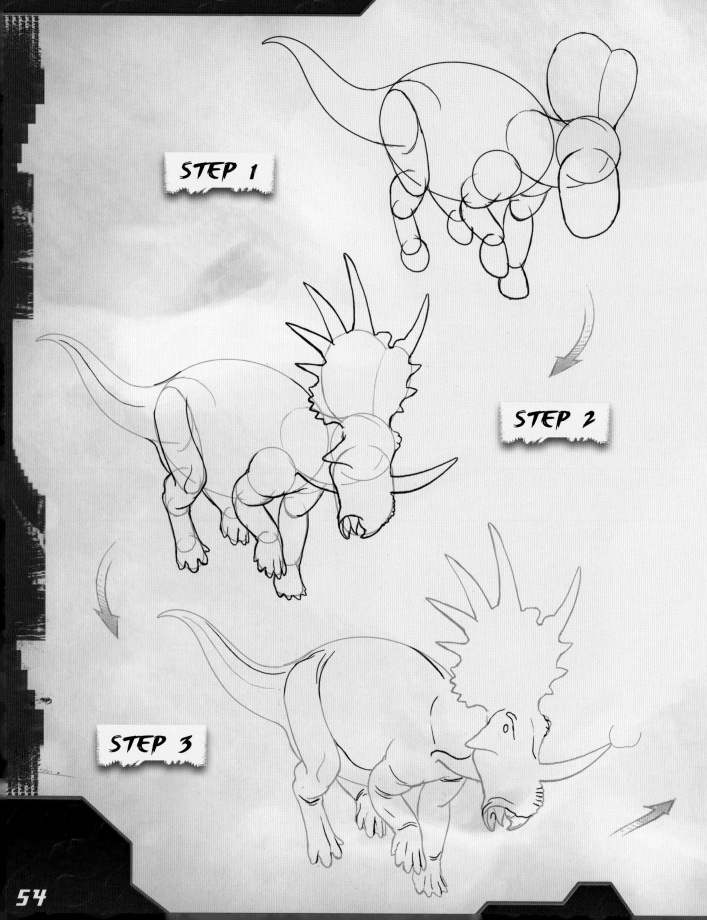

STEP 1

STEP 2

STEP 3

Styracosaurus had an unusual spiked frill at the back of its head. It also had a long horn at the top of its nose like a rhinoceros. These spikes and horn probably served as both defence tools and to attract mates. Styracosaurus was a herd dinosaur with jaws built to chop up the plants it ate.

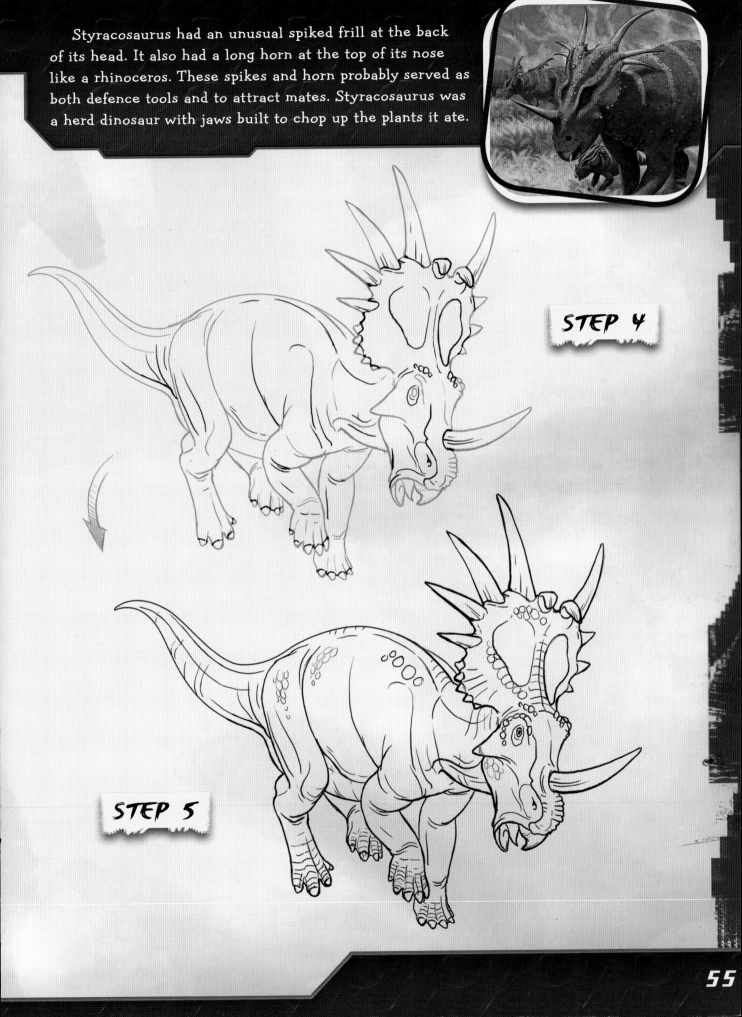

STEP 4

STEP 5

THESCELOSAURUS

STEP 1

STEP 2

STEP 3

Thescelosaurus stood on thick hind legs and was probably a swift runner. It had no teeth at the front of its jaws. Thescelosaurus may have had colouring that blended in with its surroundings to avoid predators.

STEP 4

STEP 5

TRICERATOPS
Cretaceous Period

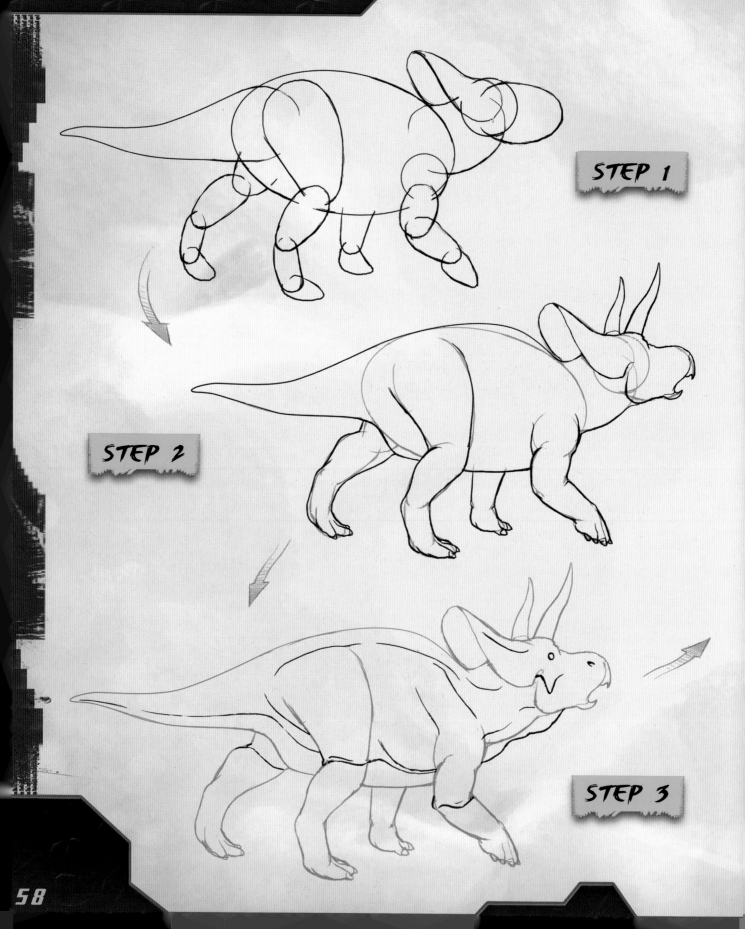

STEP 1

STEP 2

STEP 3

Triceratops was the biggest of the horned dinosaurs. It had three horns and a giant frill at the back of its head. It may have used its horns in battles against other triceratops. It ate plants. This giant dinosaur weighed between 5 and 6.5 tonnes.

STEP 4

STEP 5

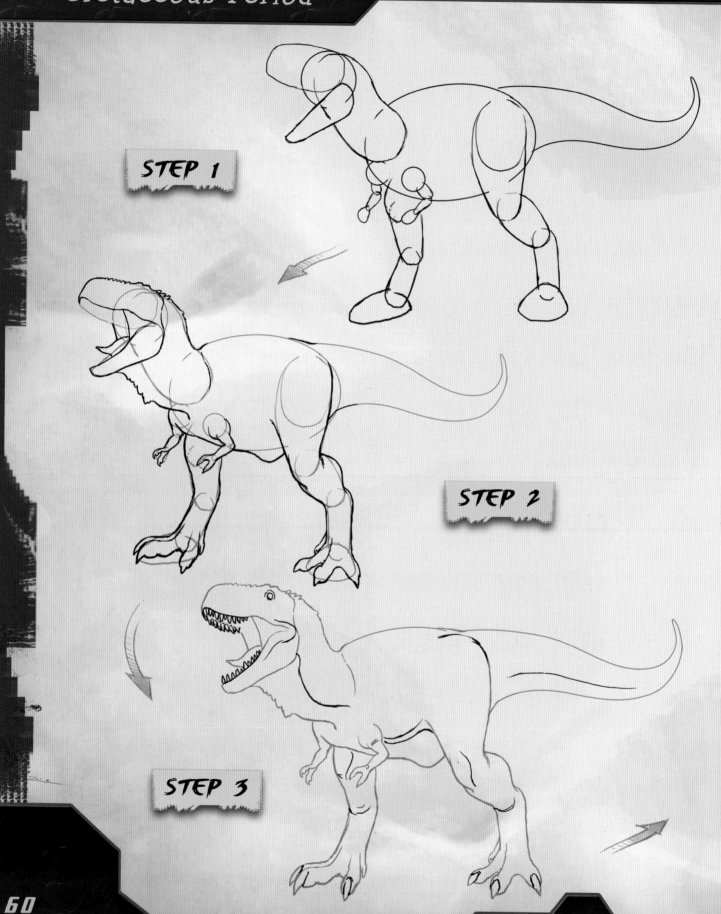

STEP 1

STEP 2

STEP 3

Tyrannosaurus rex was one of the fiercest meat-eaters to have roamed the earth. Its big teeth could slice through meat and bone. Tyrannosaurus rex would hunt and kill prey or eat dead animals it found. Scientists believe it could eat up to 45 kilograms of meat in a single bite.

STEP 4

STEP 5

VELOCIRAPTOR
Cretaceous Period

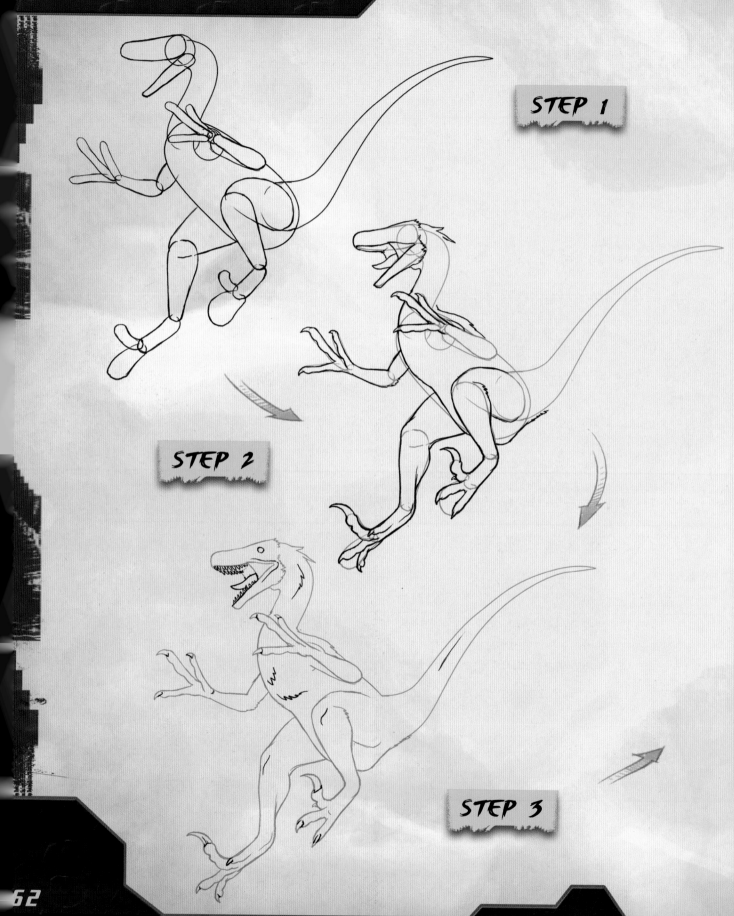

STEP 1

STEP 2

STEP 3

Velociraptor was small, fast, feathered and fierce. It had sharp, jagged teeth and a deadly claw on each hand, which it used to rip into prey. Velociraptor's long tail helped it keep its balance while attacking or fighting.

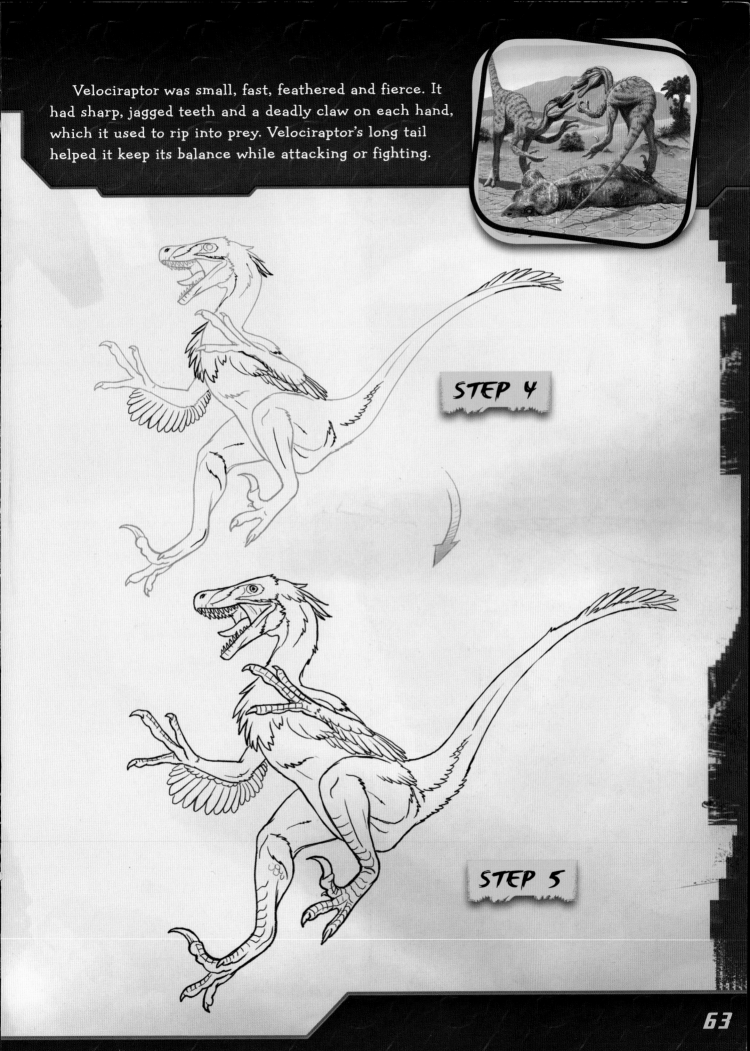

STEP 4

STEP 5

Raintree is an imprint of Capstone Global Library Limited, a company incorporated in England and Wales having its registered office at 7 Pilgrim Street, London, EC4V 6LB – Registered company number: 6695582

www.raintreepublishers.co.uk
myorders@raintreepublishers.co.uk

Text © Capstone Global Library Limited 2015
First pubished in paperback in 2014
The moral rights of the proprietor have been asserted

Printed and bound in China

ISBN 978 1 4062 8005 0
18 17 16 15 14
10 9 8 7 6 5 4 3 2 1

The name of the Smithsonian Institution and the sunburst logo are registered trademarks of the Smithsonian Institution. For more information, please visit www.si.edu Our very special thanks to Mike Brett-Surman, PhD, Museum Specialist for Fossil Dinosaurs, Reptiles, Amphibians, and Fish at the National Museum of Natural History for his curatorial review. Capstone would also like to thank Ellen Nanney and Kealy Wilson at the Smithsonian Institution's Office of Licensing for their help in the creation of this book.

Smithsonian Enterprises: Carol LeBlanc, Vice President; Brigid Ferraro, Director of Licensing

Colour Illustration credits:
Capstone: James Field, 3 (all), 5, 7, 11, 13, 15, 17, 23, 25, 27, 31, 35, 37, 39, 41, 43, 45, 49, 51, 53, 55, 57, 59, 61, 63, Steve Weston, 9, 19, 21, 29, 33, 47

British Library Cataloguing in Publication Data
A full catalogue record for this book is available from the British Library.

WEBSITES

http://kids.nationalgeographic.com/kids/games/puzzlesquizzes/brainteaserdinosaurs
How much do you really know about dinosaurs? Play this quiz to find out.

www.dragoart.com/dinosaurs-c323-1.htm
This website contains loads of different guides to help you draw more dinosaurs.

www.nhm.ac.uk/kids-only/dinosaurs
Find out some fasinating facts about dinosaurs on this website, from one of the UK's most famous museums.